A TASTE OF CHICKEN SOUP

FOR THE

CHRISTIAN FAMILY SOUL

Stories to Open the Heart and Rekindle the Spirit

Jack Canfield, Mark Victor Hansen,
Patty Aubery, Nancy Mitchell Autio

Health Communications, Inc.
Deerfield Beach, Florida

www.hcibooks.com
www.chickensoup.com

The Tablecloth. Reprinted by permission of Richard Bauman. ©1995 Richard Bauman.

Led By God. Reprinted by permission of Bill Holton. ©1999 Bill Holton.

The Wonder Years. Reprinted by permission of Mayo Mathers. ©1997 Mayo Mathers.

Luke's Truck. Reprinted by permission of Roberta L. Messner. ©1991 Roberta L. Messner.

Mrs. Tree and Her Gentleman Caller. Reprinted by permission of Sean Patrick. ©1999 Sean Patrick. Originally appeared in *Catholic Digest*.

A Child's Prayer. Reprinted by permission of Lini R. Grol ©1999 Lini R. Grol.

Heart Sounds. Reprinted by permission of Tim Madigan. ©1997 Tim Madigan. Originally appeared in the *Fort Worth Star-Telegram*, January 12, 1997.

A Rainbow's Promise Reprinted by permission of LeAnn Thieman. ©1999 LeAnn Thieman.

The Girl with the Golden Hair. Reprinted by permission of Eva Unga. ©1999 Eva Unga. Originally appeared in *Woman's World* magazine.

Waiting for the Bus. Excerpted from the *Liguorian*. Reprinted by permission of Allan Weinert, CSSR ©1997 the *Liguorian*.

Library of Congress Cataloging-in-Publication Data is on file with the Library of Congress

© 2005 Jack Canfield and Mark Victor Hansen
ISBN 0-7573-0349-8

Publisher: Health Communications Inc.
      3201 SW 15th Street, Deerfield Beach, FL 33442

With love, we dedicate this book
to our families and to all of
the Christian families around
the world.

Contents

Introduction

We believe these stories of people who chose hope over helplessness when facing a dark time, who extended a hand to someone in need, or who put their faith in God when the odds were against them, will buoy your spirits and nourish your soul. They will deepen your faith; inspire you to commit greater acts of kindness and compassion; encourage you to forgive others; remind you that you are never alone no matter how difficult your circumstances; and encourage you to see the divine love everywhere-within you and around you-every day. We are also confident that these stories will act as a blueprint in you remind, giving you models for how to more closely walk with God within the context of your immediate and extended families.

We pray that these stories will remind you of what is most important in life and

encourage you to act in accordance with
those higher priorities.

The Tablecloth

There are no hopeless situations; there are only people who have grown hopeless about them.

UNKNOWN

A young minister had been called to serve at an old church that at one time had been a magnificent edifice in a wealthy part of town. Now the area was in a state of decline and the church was in bad shape. Nevertheless, the pastor and his wife were thrilled with the church and believed they could restore it to its former magnificence.

When the minister took charge of the church early in October 1948, he and his wife immediately went to work painting, repairing and attempting to restore it. Their goal was to have the old edifice looking its best for Christmas Eve services.

Just two days before Christmas, however, a storm swept through the area, dumping more than an inch of rain. The roof of the old church sprung a leak just behind the altar. The plaster soaked up the water as if it were a sponge and then crumbled, leaving a gaping hole in the wall.

Dejected, the pastor and his wife looked at the defaced wall. There was obviously no chance to repair the damage before Christmas. Nearly three months of hard work had been washed away. Yet the young couple accepted the damage as God's will and set about cleaning up the damp debris.

It was a depressed minister and his wife who attended a benefit auction for the church youth group that afternoon. One of the items put up for bid was an old gold-and-ivory-colored lace tablecloth, nearly fifteen feet long.

Seized with an inspiration, the pastor was the high bidder at $6.50. His idea was to hang the ornate cloth behind the altar to cover the ragged hole in the wall.

On the day before Christmas, snowflakes

mingled with the howling wind. As the pastor unlocked the church doors, he noticed an older woman standing at the nearby bus stop. He knew the bus wouldn't be there for at least half an hour, so he invited her inside to keep warm.

She wasn't from the neighborhood, she explained. She had been in the area to be interviewed for a job as a governess to the children of a well-known wealthy family. She had been a war refugee, her English was poor and she didn't get the job.

Head bowed in prayer, she sat in a pew near the back of the church. She paid no attention to the pastor, who was hanging the tablecloth across the unsightly hole. When the woman looked up and saw the cloth, she rushed to the altar.

"It's mine!" she exclaimed. "It's my banquet cloth!"

Excitedly she told the surprised minister its history and even showed him her initials embroidered in one corner.

She and her husband had lived in Vienna, Austria, and had opposed the Nazis before the Second World War. They decided to flee to Switzerland, but her husband said they must go separately. She left first. Later she heard that he had died in a concentration camp.

Touched by her story, the minister insisted she take the cloth. She thought about it for a moment but said no, she didn't need it any longer, and it did look pretty hanging behind the altar. Then she said good-bye and left.

In the candlelight of the Christmas Eve services, the tablecloth looked even more magnificent. The white lace seemed dazzling in the flickering light of the candles, and the golden threads woven through it were like the brilliant rays of a new dawn.

As members of the congregation left the church, they complimented the pastor on the services and on how beautiful the church looked.

One older gentleman lingered, admiring the tablecloth, and as he was leaving he said to the minister:

"It's strange. Many years ago my wife—God rest her—and I owned such a tablecloth. She used it only on very special occasions. But we lived in Vienna then."

The night air was freezing, but the goose-bumps on the pastor's skin weren't caused by the weather. As calmly as he could, he told the man about the woman who had been to the church that very afternoon.

"Can it be," gasped the old man, tears streaming down his cheeks, "that she is alive? How can I find her?"

The pastor remembered the name of the family who had interviewed the woman. With the trembling old man at his side, he telephoned the family and learned her name and address.

In the pastor's old car they drove to her home on the other side of town. Together they knocked on her apartment door. When she opened it, the pastor witnessed the tearful, joyful and thrilling reunion of husband and wife.

Some people would call it an extremely lucky chance happening, the result of a hole in the church wall, an old tablecloth, a pastor's ingenuity in solving a problem and so on. But the combination of events was far too complex for it to have been merely "coincidence."

If one link in the fragile chain of events

had been broken, the husband and wife might never have found each other. If the rain hadn't come, if the church roof hadn't leaked, if the pastor had decided not to go to the auction, if the woman hadn't been looking for a job or standing on that corner at just the right time . . . . The list of ifs is virtually endless.

It was simply God's will. And, as it has been said many times, He works in mysterious ways.

Richard Bauman

Led by God

The desire of a man is his kindness.

PROVERBS 19:22

The car heater was running full blast, but it was still freezing cold inside the blue Oldsmobile as Monica steered onto the main road. It was a few minutes before midnight, December 31. All of the businesses were closed and every house was pitch dark. *Everyone is out celebrating,* Monica thought as yet another spasm of pain gripped her like a vise.

Across the nation millions of people were eagerly awaiting the arrival of a brand-new year. Monica, alone and terrified, had a different kind of arrival to contend with.

Twenty minutes before Monica had been warm and cozy, gabbing with friends and having a wonderful time. She and her friend Dawn were swapping pregnancy stories and trying to guess which of their babies would be the first to arrive. Both women were due in early February.

Monica, who was separated from her fiancé, was looking forward to the arrival of her second child. So was her seven-year-old daughter, Amanda. Amanda was with her grandparents now, on their way to the family's beach cottage. Monica had stopped off to spend a few minutes with friends before making the forty-five-minute drive to join them.

It was just past eleven and Monica was buttoning her coat to leave when suddenly she felt a tiny cramp in her abdomen. "Are you okay?" her friends asked, concerned.

"It was probably just a false labor pain," Monica said, refusing their offer to rush her to the hospital. "I'm not due for another five weeks yet."

But starting her car, Monica felt a second cramp, stronger than the first. *Amanda was early. Maybe this baby will be too,* she thought, and headed to her folks' house to find her sister, Terry.

A few blocks from home Monica cried out in alarm as her water broke. *Stay calm,* she told herself. *The pains are still far apart. There's plenty of time before the baby comes.*

But the house was dark. *Terry must have gone out with her boyfriend,* Monica guessed. She briefly considered running inside and calling 911, but the hospital was only twelve miles away. *I can make it easily,* she thought.

It wasn't long before Monica deeply regretted her decision to drive on. "I'm in labor!" she cried out as an intense contraction took hold and refused to let go. "I need help! I can't have this baby alone!"

Monica sped to the nearest pay phone. But the phone had been removed, and every business in sight was closed for the holiday. It was twelve o'clock midnight, and there wasn't another car on the road anywhere.

Frantic, Monica turned off the main road and steered down residential streets searching for even one house with its lights burning. *Please, God, let someone be home,* she prayed, turning into a cul-de-sac where she discovered several houses with lights and cars.

Monica pulled in front of one house, threw open the car door and struggled unsteadily to her feet. But at the last second something told her to head the other way, across the street to a different house.

The front lawn seemed as wide as a football field as Monica stumbled to the porch. "Please, someone call an ambulance!" she cried out, pressing the bell with one hand while banging on the door with the other. "I'm having a baby—right now!"

Dianne Minter, thirty-five, was awakened from a sound sleep by the sudden commotion at her mom's front door. Dianne, her husband Clyde, and their three kids had traveled all the way from Lynchburg, Virginia, through falling snow to spend New Year's Day with her parents, George and Joyce Ware. Dianne was exhausted, but the instant her mom called her name she was on her feet and racing to the stairs, still dressed in a pair of red pajamas.

"Oh my!" Dianne exclaimed when she saw the very pregnant woman all but collapsed in her dad's arms. "Lay her down so I can examine her," she instructed.

"I need an ambulance!" Monica sobbed. "I can feel my baby coming!"

"I've already called 911," Dianne's mom calmly spoke. "You certainly picked the right house to come to. My daughter is a labor and delivery nurse."

Dianne's dad gathered up sheets and blankets while her brother-in-law, Dale, a former emergency medical technician, held Monica's hand and monitored her pulse.

"I can see something coming," Dianne said after yet another contraction, only she wasn't sure it was the baby's head. When Monica visited her obstetrician just two days ago the baby had been lying sideways in her womb. Five weeks was plenty of time for the baby to shift into the proper position, the doctor had assured Monica. *But that was only two days ago,* Dianne silently worried. For Dianne knew all too well that if the baby was still transverse there was a good chance Monica might deliver an arm or a foot first, or the cord could get caught and without an emergency C-section Monica's pre-term infant might even die.

"Please don't let anything bad happen to my baby!" Monica begged, sensing something was wrong.

"Try not to push," Dianne coaxed her, hoping to delay the baby's birth until Monica could be taken to the hospital.

When the paramedics arrived, Dianne helped load Monica onto the stretcher, but it was too late to move her. "The baby's crowning!" Dianne exclaimed, greatly relieved because finally she could see the baby's head.

A few more contractions and the baby was out. A few seconds later she heard the sweetest sound in the world—her baby's first cries.

Dianne bundled the baby snugly and handed him to his mom. "Hold him close and keep him as warm as you can," she gently instructed.

"Thank you," Monica sobbed as she was carried away on the stretcher.

At the hospital the admitting nurse was about to have Monica taken to a delivery room when she heard the tiny cries. Instead she rushed the baby to a warming bed in the neonatal intensive care unit, where doctors soon pronounced baby Jacob healthy and fit as a fiddle.

The next morning Monica was cuddling her four-pound, thirteen-ounce newborn son in her arms when Dianne and her family arrived with a gift-wrapped baby outfit and rattle. Monica burst into tears the moment she spotted Dianne in the doorway.

"Thank you," she sobbed. "I know God must have led me to your house last night."

"It certainly was a New Year's Eve I'll never forget," Dianne replied.

Bill Holton
Excerpted from *Woman's World* magazine

The Wonder Years

Think big thoughts but relish small pleasures.

ANONYMOUS

One bleak day eighteen years ago, I was awash with self-pity. I was quagmired in the "terrible twos"—a parenting stage that started early and lingered long at our house—and there was no hope in sight.

The morning began with the usual activities, but I tried to rush my small sons through them. Company was coming that evening, and I wanted a clean house. I'd finished cleaning the living room and begun the family room when I heard whispered giggles coming from my boys. With a sense of foreboding, I tiptoed to the doorway and gasped in dismay at the sight before me.

"Doesn't the living room look pretty, Mommy?" Tyler, my then-four-year-old, held a giant-sized empty jar of silver glitter, while two-year-old Landon danced around in happy circles. The entire room—carpet, couch, coffee table, everything—glittered like a giant Fourth of July sparkler!

Banishing the boys to their room to play with Legos, I dragged the vacuum back into the living room. By the time it was restored to its original condition, my schedule was in shambles and I was exhausted.

Stepping up my pace, I returned to the family room. "Look, Mommy! We're helping!" my boys shrieked in delight. This time the empty container was an economy-size can of Comet cleanser I thought I had placed in a locked cabinet. I was too shocked even to gasp as I surveyed the scene before me. The floor and every book, plant, knickknack and piece of furniture were covered with a fine layer of bluish-white grit.

The worst was yet to come. The last room to be cleaned was the master bedroom that we'd recently recarpeted. As I walked into the room, my attention was immediately drawn to a large, black spot smack in the middle of the floor. Beside it sat an empty bottle of permanent black ink I'd inadvertently left out. I crumpled to my knees in tears.

That's how most of our days went during those preschool years. We bounced from disaster to disaster: perfume poured on my new satin bedspread; the phone cord cut with scissors while I was talking on the phone. If it could be poured, dumped, sprinkled or sprayed, Tyler and Landon found a way to do it. There was no shelf the two of them could not reach, no lid they could not pry off.

After I discovered the ink spot that morning, I called my mom, but she didn't provide the sympathy I expected. "Honey, I know it feels as though this time will never end but believe me, a blink of your eye and it'll be gone. You have to find a way to cherish this season of your life."

This is not what I want to hear, I thought. But I knew she was right. I just didn't know how to switch from surviving to cherishing. So from that morning on, I asked God for help. And in the process, I became aware of some patterns that had squashed my capacity for joy. Life in the Mathers home lightened up as I worked to change some of my habits.

First, I realized I overused the word "no." Some days it seemed I'd forgotten how to say "yes." One afternoon I jotted down everything to which I regularly responded "no." Looking over the completed list, I discovered I denied far too many of my sons' requests because they would make a mess or take too much time.

For example, the boys loved to pull their chairs to the kitchen sink and play in the water while I did dishes, but this slowed me down and made a sudsy mess. I decided to remove this activity from my "no" list.

The next morning, to the boys' delight, I filled the sink with warm water and told them to bring their chairs and have fun. This simple activity kept them so entertained, I finished my morning chores in record time.

Removing just this one "no" made a tremendous difference. The boys thought I was wonderful, and I was pretty impressed with them. As a bonus, my kitchen was cleaner than ever, thanks to all the splashed water.

But avoiding the word "no" hasn't always been easy. As Tyler and Landon grew older, I discovered that overusing it made them feel untrustworthy. The first time Landon asked to go camping overnight with friends, I refused to consider it. He angrily accused me of not trusting him. Although Landon was wrong, I couldn't really explain the fear that made me deny his request.

When my husband suggested my refusal was based on a reluctance to let Landon grow up, I knew he was right. We sat down together and laid out clear plans for the campout. Landon had a great time and I survived, thanks to several calls he made from a pay phone to reassure me he was okay. Several weeks later, when he asked to go to an unsupervised party, I again declined. This time Landon was disappointed, but not angry. He knew I trusted him—just not the circumstances.

I also realized I didn't laugh enough. Proverbs 15:15 promises that "a cheerful heart has a continual feast." During the preschool years, however, I was becoming emotionally anorexic. I'd forgotten there's something humorous to be found in almost every situation.

After one particularly trying day with my preschoolers, I escaped to a long, steamy shower, leaving my husband to oversee the boys. I'd just dressed when our neighbor dropped by for coffee. As she followed me to the kitchen, she stopped abruptly.

"Interesting," she murmured, studying the dining room floor. "We've always kept our catsup in the refrigerator." I followed her gaze to a giant red puddle circled neatly on the carpet. Husband and sons were nowhere to be seen. Instant embarrassment and anger inflated my chest. Then I caught the twinkle in my neighbor's eyes, and we both burst into laughter. Laughing can help shrink things down to manageable proportions.

I've definitely needed that healthy dose of humor in each stage of parenting. Learning to find the humor in difficult or embarrassing situations has often defused tension.

I compared my kids and my parenting to others. I routinely measured my success as a parent by this faulty yardstick—and came up short. As I scrutinized my friends' choices, I constantly second-guessed mine.

My insecurities increased as the boys grew older. One afternoon I was waiting in line to pick them up from school when I noticed a bumper sticker on the car in front of mine: "My child is an honor student at Pilot Butte School." Glancing around, I saw another vehicle with a similar sticker, then another.

Suddenly, it seemed my car was the only one lacking a badge of success!

My temptation to compare raged strongest when it was time for my sons to pursue plans beyond high school. As I listened to other parents talk about the colleges to which their kids were applying or the scholarships they were receiving, my insecurities blossomed. I found myself being apologetic about Tyler's plans to work before going to school. Not until I caught the same tone in Tyler's voice did I realize I was passing my insecurities to him. That was the last thing I wanted to bequeath my son. Asking God's forgiveness, I determined to focus squarely on God—not on other people. That decision is one that I still renew every morning when I ask God for help.

Now as the parent of grown children, I see my mother was right. The preschool years passed in the blink of an eye. But it wasn't just those years that vanished in a moment— it was all of childhood! One moment we were reading Mother Goose together, the next, it was college catalogs.

As my sons have matured, I've found that everyday traumas that accompany each parenting stage come with valuable lessons. That became clear to me the day I found the ink on my new carpet. I called every cleaner in town for advice on removing the stain. The only solution was to cover it with a rug.

I just couldn't accept that. I had to try something. Getting a basin of water and a washcloth, I began soaking up the ink and rinsing out the cloth. Soaking . . . rinsing . . . soaking . . . rinsing. As I worked, tears spilling down my cheeks, chubby little hands patted me on the back.

"We're sorry, Mommy," they said. While Tyler ran to get more water, Landon brought a bar of soap. Together we worked and gradually, before our disbelieving eyes, the spot that should have been permanent disappeared.

That day I discovered God looks on mothers with a special kind of love. He knows our insecurities, our frustrations, our desire to be good parents. And sometimes, when we need it most, He goes out of his way to prove his love. Tucked away with my cleaning supplies is a reminder of that. It's the cloth I used to clean the carpet. To this day it remains stained with permanent black ink!

Mayo Mathers

Luke's Truck

God's finger touched him, and he slept.
ALFRED LORD TENNYSON

Eyes wide with terror peered at me from the hospital bed. "You must be Luke Hatten," I said, as I scanned the name on his identification bracelet. His work-roughened hands nervously fingered a pamphlet. Its bold, red letters shrieked *When You Have Cancer*.

I cleared my throat uneasily. "I'm Roberta Messner, a registered nurse. Your doctor and wife thought it might be helpful if I visit you when you're discharged. If it's okay, I'll stop by Saturday."

Mr. Hatten stared blankly out the

window at the barren view. In a couple of months, the hospital grounds would be awash with a carpet of crocuses, vibrant azaleas and hyacinths in Easter-egg hues. But this was the cancer ward, where time is measured in moments—not months.

Mr. Hatten's roommate caught up with me by the elevator. "You've got your work cut out for you, Nurse," he stated flatly. "They say it's terminal. Ever since Luke got his sentence, he walks the floor all night. He told me, 'I can't sit for long. When I sit, I think.'"

I felt whipped from the start. Here it was the eve of spring, with the promise of new life, and *my* patient was dying. How could I help him?

On Saturday morning, a short, stout woman met me at the door of the Hattens' tidy rural cottage. "I'm Ida. Do come in," she said, tugging the hem of her apron.

Luke sat in a frayed wing chair in a corner of the living room. He forced a smile. Just two weeks before, Luke had undergone surgery for colon cancer. But the relentless disease had spread. Once a hard-working handyman, a now-weary Luke clutched his abdomen in a spasm of pain. *Lord, help me know what to do*, I silently prayed.

"Luke just took a pain pill," Ida explained. "Why don't we have some coffee out in the kitchen while the medicine takes hold?" I followed her to the gingham-curtained kitchen window. A look of desperation stole across her deeply-lined face. "This is all such a shock," she said, tearing up. "He worked so hard—always tinkerin' on something. And just when he thought he was ready to retire, *this* happens."

Ida bit her lip, then pointed to the shining red truck in the driveway. "He wanted that truck so bad. Drove it straight from the showroom over to the clinic. His belly had been painin' him a little, but we never dreamed it was . . . cancer. Next day, the doc just cut him open and sewed him right back up."

I walked back into the living room. "That's quite a truck you have out there, Luke," I said.

"Never even got to show it to the crew down at the hardware store," came his faint words. "Doc says I can't drive. I'm on too many pills."

"Sometime when you feel up to some fresh air, I'd love to take a look at it. My husband has a truck, too, but it's an old clunker."

Luke's brown eyes lit up. "Had old junk heaps all of my life. Always kept hopin' to get a new one. Then I did—just before this thing hit." He struggled out of the chair and pressed a kiss to Ida's cheek. "Gimme my coat, Hon."

With marrow-deep determination, Luke led me to the driveway. He pointed to a row of brittle, lifeless bushes. "There'll be yellow blossoms like you never did see on them come spring. Sure would like to see spring come one more time." Dusting the glistening truck with the sleeve of his plaid flannel jacket, he cautiously peeped in the windows as if it belonged to someone else.

"Would my husband ever love this beauty!" I exclaimed. "Just look at those chrome bumpers and black leather seats."

"Well, climb up in 'er and have a seat," he urged. Luke settled himself behind the steering wheel, reaching in his pocket for keys. "Feels funny not havin' a floorboard full of old rags and oil cans," he chuckled.

"Better start it up to charge the battery," I suggested.

Luke turned the key in the ignition. "Gotta let it run a minute to lube the engine," he explained, honking the horn with the fervor of a three-year-old.

A neighbor tapped on the window. "Hey Luke, what's a pretty young nurse doing in that truck of yours?" he chided.

Luke toyed with the power seats, the electric mirrors, the quartz clock, the heater. My idle hands longed for a stethoscope. A thermometer. *Anything* to avoid the inevitable discussion. But all my gadgets were in the Hattens' living room.

"How'd you ever decide on the color, Luke?" I asked, opting for small talk.

"Same color as the bike I got the Christmas I turned seven. Pa made me wait 'til after supper to ride it up the holler. Seemed like forever."

Once in the driver's seat, Luke emerged strong, in control, and finally opened up to me. "One day I was drivin' this truck off the car lot, and the next thing I knew, they were sendin' a nurse to help me die," he said softly. I nodded and reached for his hand.

"Doc says I don't have long. I gotta put things in order, Nurse. I'm tellin' you this 'cause I don't wanna worry Ida."

I visited Luke several times each week. He'd be waiting in the driver's seat with a thermos of coffee and two mugs. We talked freely of our shared faith, his fear of dying and leaving Ida alone, and God's promise of eternal life. As Luke learned to face his pain, he grew more peaceful. After our "truck talks," we'd head back to the kitchen where Ida waited. There we'd discuss the details of Luke's care and help Ida prepare for an uncertain future.

On Palm Sunday, I attended church before checking on Luke. The pastor spoke about how Jesus became a man so that we could know God. He closed with the story of Jesus facing death in the Garden of Gethsemane. Jesus had told his disciples: "My soul is exceedingly sorrowful, even unto death: tarry ye here, and watch with me." (Matthew 26:38) Even Jesus had not wanted to face death alone.

That afternoon I found Luke leaning on Ida by a budding forsythia bush. His old leather belt curled about him, gathering his trousers in loose folds. He handed me some freshly cut branches, wrapped in wet paper towels and newspapers. "Put these in a jug of water when you go home, and they'll take root. Someday you'll have a yard full of forsythias."

I smiled, but deep down I doubted his wisdom. With what little I knew about gardening, I was sure a budding branch had a slim chance of taking root.

Over the next few days, Luke's condition rapidly worsened. At our last visit, he lay ashen and listless, his breathing rapid and labored. I leaned over to give him a hug.

"I'm not afraid anymore," he whispered. "Jesus is right here, reachin' his arms out to me. I'll live again . . . just like my Lord."

Luke died that evening. I drove over to be with Ida. "Oh, how I'll miss him," she wept. "But how could I drag my Luke back to this Earth? He's livin' with Jesus. One day I'll see him."

As I left their home, I paused by Luke's truck. Gazing into the window, I studied the empty seats where the two of us had so often sat. The air was fragrant with the scent of spring flowers. With the sleeve of my sweater, I buffed the red gem as Luke would have done, then lifted the windshield wipers to release a wayward cluster of golden forsythia blossoms.

To really make a difference in the lives of others, we have to meet them where they are, I thought. I might never have known the real Luke in his bewildering, antiseptic hospital room—my secure environment. There, in the rush, I might have patted his hand, offered reassurance and gone on about my duties.

But sipping coffee in that truck—Luke's Garden of Gethsemane—the barriers were broken. Two strangers experienced the promise of Easter.

If I ever forget that, I'm reminded each spring by my yard full of Luke's forsythias.

Roberta L. Messner

Mrs. Tree and Her Gentleman Caller

God has given us two hands—one to receive with and the other to give with.

REVEREND BILLY GRAHAM

Mrs. Tree had lived alone since becoming a widow a quarter-century before. Like most people in our neighborhood, she had little. But what she did have was enough for her meager needs—rent, a little food, electricity and a donation each week to her church.

But she had not attended services for some time. Mrs. Tree was almost blind and, once her husband died, could not manage the two-block walk alone. One of her friends did her shopping, and Mrs. Tree's occasional trips to the doctor were made possible by a visiting nurse who came and picked her up.

We called her Mrs. Tree because her German name, *Baum*, she told us, meant tree. "*Tannenbaum* is a Christmas tree," she taught me patiently when I delivered papers with my brother Kevin on his paper route, "and *Rosenbaum* means rose tree."

Kevin had met the old woman one day while collecting for his route. She was sitting on a back stoop enjoying the sun. Of course she had no need for a newspaper, but Kevin's outright friendliness did not depend on whether one was a customer.

"What do you do by yourself, Mrs. Tree?" he asked, realizing how lonely she was.

"I listen to my radio," she replied. "I love some of the stories on it, like *Ma Perkins* and *Helen Trent*. Then there is fine music in the evenings or sometimes a play or a show with that funny gentleman and that little wooden puppet, Charlie McCarthy."

To be sure, Mrs. Tree was a proud woman who seldom asked for help with anything. But Kevin had a way about him that invited confidences, and, one day after finishing his paper route, he announced he was accompanying Mrs. Tree to church on Sunday.

"You'll have your hands full!" Mama laughed. "I still remember when the Ladies' Guild went to see if they could help her and she told them to mind their own business!"

Mrs. Tree, Mama added, had been a very attractive woman; her husband, a dapper gentleman, had worked for the gas company in the office. Though they were not wealthy, they enjoyed a social life, and Mrs. Tree sort of considered herself the belle of the ball.

"Perhaps," Mama speculated with a light laugh, "being helped by ladies was not her cup of tea!"

"She seems nice enough to me," Kevin said quietly.

I giggled, secretly referring to the coming Sunday as "Kev's date."

When the first church date grew into a second and then, a third, Kevin showed no sign of quitting. Nor did Mrs. Tree. Each Sunday, she'd be ready and waiting, dressed in her best, for the walk to church. For his part, Kevin, in his Sunday clothes, would help her with her coat—which she always wore, even in the heat of summer.

All the way to church, Mrs. Tree clung lightly to Kevin's arm. Once inside, she insisted on sitting in front where she'd sat with her husband.

When Kevin led Mrs. Tree out of the church, the crowd on the sidewalks parted politely. They did not, however, disguise their interest in seeing the mysterious parishioner on the arm of my older brother.

During the week, Kevin told us that Mrs. Tree had invited him in for tea and they'd sat at a comfortable old table covered with a linen cloth. They drank the tea from china cups, he said, and ate little cookies made of shortbread. Kevin promised to ask Mrs. Tree next time if he could bring some cookies home for us to enjoy, too. The dates continued through the summer and into fall.

Though Kevin was not very talkative about his friendship with the elderly widow, he did confide that she often told him stories of her husband and how they had wished for children but had not been so blessed. She also showed him photographs of herself and her husband in their younger days. Kevin told us she was a "Corker indeed," which meant, in his practiced eye, she was very attractive.

As the leaves began to fall in earnest, Mrs. Tree seemed to slow a bit. Kev said she remarked more often about "these tired old bones" and how the winter days seemed to hang in her loneliness.

"I'll still come here for you!" Kevin protested. "And my brothers can come, too."

She smiled and told him he was a kind lad, and she thanked God for bringing him to help her.

As Kevin got up to leave, Mrs. Tree pointed out a crumb on his lip and handed him a handkerchief. He dabbed his lip and went to the door, absentmindedly taking with him the lace-bordered cloth.

"I forgot to give her the hanky!" he said, still clutching the sweet-smelling linen when he got home.

"How did she know you had a crumb there," Mama asked, "with no eyes to see?"

Kevin stood thunderstruck. He turned to go out the door, intent on returning the hanky. But Mama told him she thought perhaps it was all right to stay put, and so he stashed the handkerchief in his drawer, planning to return it on Sunday.

A few days later, Father O'Phelan informed us that Mrs. Tree had passed on the night before. Mama, though, was not surprised when we brought her the news. Indeed, she seemed to think that the handkerchief was the old woman's way of saying good-bye to my brother.

A funeral was held on Saturday morning, and Kevin sat next to Mama in the pew usually reserved for family. He was, for what it was worth, all she had.

It turned out that, shortly before she died, Mrs. Tree had bundled a few books and an old framed picture of her and her late husband with a note to give the items to Kevin. But the remembrance he cherished most was the old woman's sweet-smelling handkerchief. It was, he's said in the years since, her personal good-bye and a thank you far and above anything he ever expected.

Sean Patrick

A Child's Prayer

The family that prays together, stays together!

AL SCALPONE

"Don't you remember me, Nurse?"

When people ask me if I remember them, I get a sinking feeling in my stomach. This was no exception. I was new to that particular school district, but I'd been all over Amsterdam doing school nursing as well as public health and infant childcare. How was I to remember all those mothers over the years?

I must have shown my embarrassment at not recognizing this mother. She chuckled before she said: "I don't blame you, Nurse, for it was so long ago that we met. You were still a student nurse working in the barracks with the diphtheria patients, and you nursed my son, Henk, then only five years old."

"Yes, oh yes. I remember my little Henky." He'd been such a lovable little boy, but so very sick when he came from the holiday camp. He'd been homesick and sad, being so far away from home.

My training-school hospital was close to the seaside and we often treated children from these camps. That was before the war. Yes, I remembered Henky, and even his mother . . . only too well.

His files had said that he was Roman Catholic, so that night I prayed with him before and after supper and again just before I tucked him in for the night. I slept in the barracks, too, and my bedroom window looked out on the children in the glass cubicles. He was only one of ten patients, one I never forgot. His throat was very sore; therefore, I didn't think too much of it that he didn't pray with me or say the responses. Nevertheless, I kept on praying with him for several days. One day, he began to talk.

But even though he folded his little hands and closed his eyes devoutly when I told him that we were going to pray, he never prayed with me.

One day I asked him: "Come on, Henky, pray with me; you know how, don't you?"

His big blue eyes looked up at me earnestly, and he only shrugged. I thought then that he'd forgotten about prayer, since he was in strange surroundings and it was not a Christian camp. One had to keep reminding the children; otherwise they would forget to pray, I'd thought.

From then on, Henky prayed with me—haltingly at first. But soon he was most eager to pray. Before long he was leading me in the Lord's Prayer and soon he was proud to say all the prayers by himself.

Travel was expensive, and it was difficult for the parents to visit. One day his mother came for a visit. She could not come in and had to talk to Henky through the window on the veranda. They shouted back and forth most cheerfully, and I smiled to myself when I heard Henky boast about his prayers. He was indeed a religious boy, never forgetting his prayers—even at naptime. It was always a moving moment when I saw his little hands folded and his eyes closed as he knelt beside his bed. I hoped his mother would stay to see him at his prayers.

Suddenly an angry knocking at the door startled me. I, too, was in quarantine, so I could only talk to the visitors from a distance. It was Henky's mother. Her eyes flashed as she snapped: "Who told you to teach Henky to pray?"

It was obvious that she objected to prayer—and strongly. "But he is Christian," I said lamely. "It is on his files."

She snorted angrily: "That's his father, of course. He filled in the forms and he had to write that down even though he never goes to church or prays."

I wanted to comfort her and said timidly: "A little prayer never did any harm."

"No, of course not," she agreed hesitantly. Then with a rueful smile she added: "That'll put him to shame when Henky comes home with prayers of his own." She shrugged and said almost sadly: "It won't last though; Henky's too small to keep it up. And no one will encourage him—certainly not his father. As for me. . . ." She turned around in mid-sentence and stomped off.

She hadn't told me to stop praying, and so Henky and I cheerfully went on praying and singing the religious songs. My parents prayed and sang for every reason or season. It was part of our life. Henky loved to sing and pray, and soon he knew my whole repertoire.

When his parents came to take him home, he cried—much to their amazement. Yes, I remembered Henky.

All that flashed through my mind as I looked at the woman before me. Eleven years had gone by. I had often thought of Henky, but only as the five-year-old.

"How is Henky?" I asked eagerly.

His mother laughed. "You should see him. Thin and tall—a marvelous boy. Everybody loves him. He always talks about you."

She put a hand on my arm and said earnestly: "But you did something quite wonderful when you gave Henk religion."

I wanted to protest that I had done very little in the six weeks he was with me. But she was so excited, she gave me no time to speak. She had come to see me to tell her story and was bursting to share it.

I listened in amazement as she continued. "You know, I never expected Henky's prayers to last. But he kept up and taught his little sisters to pray as well. He wouldn't eat or go to sleep without his prayers. By that time, my husband felt that he should go to a Christian school and the girls as well. Soon we both joined the children when they prayed.

"Then the war came, and we needed prayer to give sense to our lives and our suffering. We prayed and sang together as Henky taught us day after day.

"Needless to say, we all joined the church and were strengthened in our most difficult times. God has been good to us. He must have sent Henky your way to get us all into his stable. Henky's prayers went a long way."

Lini R. Grol

Heart Sounds

A bone to the dog is not charity. Charity is the bone shared with the dog when you are just as hungry as the dog.

JACK LONDON

One afternoon about a week before Christmas, my family of four piled into our minivan to run a short errand, and this question came from a small voice in the back seat: "Dad," began my five-year-old son, Patrick, "how come I've never seen you cry?"

Just like that. No preamble. No warning. One minute it's, "Mom, what's for supper?" The next it's, "Dad, how come . . ." My wife, Catherine, was as surprised by this as me. But she is one of those lucky souls for whom

tears come naturally; are spilled sponta-
neously then quickly forgotten. Patrick has
seen his mother cry dozens of times. So my
wife was entitled to turn my way in the
front passenger seat with a mischievous
smile that said, "Explain this one, Dad." I
couldn't, of course. I mumbled something in
reply about crying when my son was not
around, at sad movies and so forth. But I
knew immediately that Patrick had put his
young finger on the largest obstacle to my
own peace and contentment, i.e., the
dragon-filled moat separating me from the
fullest human expression of joy, sadness,
anger and disappointment. Simply put, I
could not cry.

I know I am scarcely the only man for
whom this is true. In fact I believe that tear-
less men are the rule in our society, not the
exception. When, for instance, did John
Wayne shed tears, or Kirk Douglas, or any of
those other Hollywood archetypes of man-
liness? For instance, Wayne's best buddy
has been slain on the battlefield and The
Duke looks down to the body of his fallen
friend with studied sobriety, but also with
his typical calm. Then he moves on to the

next battle with his typical bravado.

We men. We fathers and sons have been condemned to follow Wayne's lead. Passing centuries have conditioned us to believe that stoicism is the embodiment of strength, and unfettered emotion that of weakness. We have feigned imperviousness to the inevitable slings and arrows, traveling through life with stiff upper lips, calm on the outside, secretly dying within.

A recent television news report only confirmed what I have long suspected. According to the news, the number of men being diagnosed with depression today is skyrocketing. But I submit that we men have always been depressed to one degree or another, though we tend to medicate it with alcohol, or work, or afternoons and evenings sitting mindlessly in front of one televised sports event or another.

Take me, for instance. For most of my adult life I have battled chronic depression, an awful and insidious disorder that saps life of its color and meaning, and too often leads to self-destruction. Doctors have said much of my problem is physiological, an inherited chemical imbalance, something akin to diabetes. Those physicians have treated it as such with medication.

But I also know that much of my illness is attributable to years of swallowing my rage, my sadness, even my joy. Strange as it seems, in this world where macho is everything, drunkenness and depression are safer ways for men like me to deal with feelings than tears.

In my own battle, I had begun to see the folly of this long ago, well before my son's penetrating backseat query. I could only hope the same debilitating handicap would not be passed on to the generation that followed mine.

Hence our brief conversation on the sunny December afternoon after Patrick's question. He and I were back in the van after playing together at a park near our home. Before pulling out, I turned to my son and thanked him for his curiosity of the day before. Tears were a very good thing for boys and girls alike, I said. Crying is God's way of healing people when they are sad.

"I'm very glad you can cry whenever you're sad or whenever you're angry." I said. "Sometimes daddies have a harder time showing how they feel. You know, Patrick, I wish I were more like you in that way. Someday I hope I do better.

Patrick nodded. But in truth, I held out little hope. Lifelong habits are hard to break. I was sure it would take something on the order of a miracle for me to connect with the dusty core of my own emotions.

From the time he was an infant, my son has enjoyed an unusual passion and affinity for music. By age four, he could pound out several bars of Wagner's *Ride of the Valkyries* by ear on the piano. More recently, he has spent countless hours singing along with the soundtrack to the *Hunchback of Notre Dame*, happily directing the music during the most orchestral parts. But these were hidden pleasures for him, enjoyed in the privacy of his own room or with the small and forgiving audience of his mother, father and older sister, Melanie.

What the youth director of our church was suggesting was something different altogether.

"I was wondering if Patrick would sing a verse of 'Away in the Manger' during the early service on Christmas Eve." Juli Bail, the youth director, asked on our telephone answering machine.

My son's first solo. My wife and I struggled to contain our own excitement and anxiety. Catherine delicately broached the possibility, gently prodding Patrick after Juli's call, reminding him how beautifully he sang, telling him how much fun it would be. Patrick himself seemed less convinced. His face crinkled into a frown.

"You know, Mom," he said. "Sometimes when I have to do something important. I get kind of scared."

Grown-ups feel that way, too, he was quickly assured, but the decision to sing on Christmas Eve was left to him. Should Patrick choose to postpone his singing debut, that would be fine with his parents. His deliberations took only a few minutes.

"Okay," Patrick said. "I'll do it."

For the next week, Patrick practiced his stanza several times with his mother. A formal rehearsal at the church had also gone exceedingly well, my wife reported. But I could only envision myself at age five, singing into a microphone before hundreds of people. When Christmas Eve arrived, my expectations of my son's performance were limited indeed.

My son's solo came late in the service. By then, the spirit of the evening, and many beautiful performances by young voices had served to thaw my inner reaches, like a Minnesota snow bank on a sunny day in March.

Then Patrick and his young choir took the stage. Catherine, Melanie and I sat with the congregation in darkness as a spotlight found my son, standing alone at the microphone. He was dressed in white and wore a pair of angel wings, and he sang that night as if he had done so forever.

Patrick hit every note, slowly, confidently, and for those few moments, as his five-year-old voice washed over the people, he seemed transformed, a true angel, bestower of Christmas miracles. There was eternity in Patrick's voice that night, a penetrating beauty rich enough to dissolve centuries of manly reserve. At the sound of my son, heavy tears welled at the corners of my eyes, and spilled down my cheeks.

His song was soon over and the congregation applauded. Catherine brushed away tears. Melanie, my daughter, sobbed next to me. Others wept, too. After the service, I moved quickly to congratulate Patrick, but found he had more urgent priorities. "Mom," he said as his costume was stripped away. "I really have to go to the bathroom."

So Patrick disappeared. As he did, my friend and pastor, Dick Lord, wished me a Merry Christmas. But emotion choked off my reply as the two of us embraced. Outside the sanctuary in our crowded gathering place, I received congratulations from fellow church members. But I had no time to bask there in Patrick's reflected glory. I knew I had only a short window in which to act only a few minutes before my natural stoicism closed around my heart. I found my son as he emerged from the church bathroom.

"Patrick, I need to talk to you about something." I said, sniffling.

Alarm crossed his face. "Is it something bad?" he asked.

"No, it's not something bad." I answered.

"Is it something good?"

I took him by the hand and led him down a long hallway, into a darkened room where we could be alone. I knelt to his height and admired his young face in the shadows, the large blue eyes, the dusting of freckles on his nose and cheeks, the dimples on one side.

He looked at my moist eyes quizzically, with concern.

"Patrick, do you remember when you asked me why you had never seen me cry?" I began.

He nodded.

"Well, I'm crying now, aren't I?" I said.

He nodded again.

"Why are you crying, Dad?"

"Your singing was so pretty it made me cry."

Patrick smiled proudly and flew into my arms. I began to sob.

"Sometimes," my son said into my shoulder, "life is just so beautiful you have to cry."

Our moment together was over too soon, for it was Christmas Eve, and untold treasures awaited our five-year-old beneath the tree at home. But I wasn't ready for the traditional plunge into Christmas giving just yet. I handed my wife the keys to the van and set off alone for the mile-long hike from church to our home.

The night was cold and crisp. I crossed a small park and admired the full moon hanging low over a neighborhood brightly lit in the colors of the season. As I left the park and turned up a street toward home, I met a car moving slowly down the street, a family taking in the area's Christmas lights. Someone inside rolled down a backseat window.

"Merry Christmas," a child's voice yelled out to me.

"Merry Christmas," I yelled back, and the tears began to flow once again.

Tim Madigan

A Rainbow's Promise

Strangers are friends that you have yet to meet.

ROBERTA LIEBERMAN

"MaiLy! Wake up, little one!" the nun said in a frantic whisper.

MaiLy rubbed her sleepy eyes with the back of her hand. "Wake! Hurry!" Sister Katrine grasped her arm and pulled her to a sitting position. "It's time!"

Time for what? Mai wondered as she obediently stood beside her cot and watched Sister wake the other nine-year-olds in the same way. She nudged them toward Mai, then to the door and into the black night. Explosions sounded in the distance.

Whimpering children from other cottages rushed past them down the dirt path. Mai ran with them to the main gate of the orphanage where they shivered in silence. They heard the familiar rumble of Vietnamese army vehicles, then gunfire blasts nearby. Huddling closer, they wrapped their arms around each other as tanks thundered past the gate. The vibration shook through their bones. Repeated gunfire blazed sudden bursts of light against a pitch-black curtain of night as the explosions grew nearer. The trembling children cried softly. Sister Katrine opened the gate a few inches.

"The war is here, my children. Do not be afraid. God will save us but we must run for safety now." One by one she coaxed the frightened children out the gate and commanded them to run to the convent at the top of the hill. "Run!" she yelled as she shoved Mai through the gate.

Run! Run! Run! Mai commanded herself as her bare feet pounded the earth. Bombs exploded like fireworks, providing the only light as she stumbled along the rocky path. The sky became brighter as the bombing increased, but smoke clouded her way. She tried to suppress the sobs that spent her diminishing breath.

Run! Run! Run! she repeated to herself. Her tears tasted like dirt as she wiped them with her grimy hand. When she reached the convent, she ascended the stairs two at a time, then crouched in the corner and waited for the other children.

Soon an army truck pulled up. "Come! Hurry!" the nun commanded. A Vietnamese soldier pulled back the canvas canopy and boosted the children into the back of the truck two and three at a time. When the bench seats were full, the remaining children crowded together on the floor. The truck lunged forward and their treacherous journey to freedom began. Mai cuddled closer to her friends and wondered if she would see the orphanage, or the American who had promised to come back for her, ever again.

The truck snaked its way through the chaos of war and eventually to a coastal city. There the nuns and children sought refuge in a church. Hesitantly, Sister Katrine approached Mother Superior and told her of her plan to leave with MaiLy.

"Absolutely not!" the older nun hissed.

But Sister Katrine insisted. "I must try to get her to Saigon, then to the American GI who has waited for seven years to adopt her." Looking into her superior's eyes she repeated firmly, "With or without your consent, I am taking MaiLy."

With the sun setting to her back, Sister Katrine gripped Mai's hand and raced eastward toward the shore. Her habit hiked to her knees, Sister Katrine assisted in building a tiny raft, then a dozen frantic people crowded on. As their rig pushed off at sunset and drifted into the South China Sea, they looked back at a city on fire.

Sister placed MaiLy in a cardboard box, but it was flimsy protection against the tempestuous sea. Wind and mountainous waves lashed at the raft, threatening to consume it and the refugees on board. The deafening roar drowned out hollered commands and prayers. For hours the ruthless waves battered their bodies relentlessly and they fought to keep from being devoured by the monstrous sea. The sun's slow descent on the horizon seemed to steal the power from the storm. Then a vibrant rainbow appeared. "That's a sign of God's promise," Sister whispered to MaiLy. "He will protect you from life's storms."

Days later, the raft docked in Saigon. Sister Katrine and MaiLy joined the throngs of panicking people in overloaded carts, and on oxen and scooters racing for their freedom. Miraculously, Sister Katrine found the agency that had wanted to facilitate Mai's adoption. There, Sister squatted to Mai's level. "Do you remember the special American GI who came to visit you many times at the orphanage?" Mai nodded. "He lives far away. If I leave you here they will take you to him."

"But I don't want you to leave me," Mai whimpered, stepping closer to her.

Sister took a handkerchief from her sleeve and wiped her eyes. "Haven't I always taken good care of you, MaiLy?"

Mai nodded again.

"Now I can take the best care of you by letting you go."

Mai wrapped her arms around Sister Katrine's neck.

Sister whispered, "Remember, God will

take care of you—and will give you rain-bows after the storms." Then she took Mai's hand and led her to the steps of the orphan evacuation center. Mai waved good-bye to the only family she had ever known.

The next day, she was loaded on board a gutted cargo jet with one hundred other children. Babies were placed two and three to a cardboard box with toddlers and older children sitting on the side bench seats. As the plane lifted off the ground, Mai pressed her face against the window. Her tears trickled down the glass.

Babies gently bumped against each other when the plane landed in the Philippines. All the children were escorted in open-air buses to Clark Air Force Base. Mai leaned her head against the window and gazed solemnly at the scenery. The palm trees seemed to wave a tranquility unknown in Vietnam.

There was no congestion of carts, scooters or oxen.

No thunderous bombings.

No hordes of frightened people.

But also no orphanage.

No Sister Katrine.

No American GI.

Mai spent most of the next two days curled up on her mattress at Operation Babylift headquarters. Hundreds of children ran merrily and joined in games as they waited for a larger, safer plane to complete their journey. Mai lay curled, ignoring the kind acts of her volunteer caregivers. Feeling betrayed and abandoned, she wondered if she would ever see her friends, her homeland or the American GI again. She recalled the day, when she was three, that she saw him the first time. It was then she had chosen him. Clinging to his leg, she sat on his foot for a "ride" as he diapered and fed the babies. She closed her eyes and remembered swinging on his lap on the old rope swing in the dusty playground. She could almost feel his whiskers on her face as she did when she pressed her cheek to his in their usual hug. A smile crossed her lips as she relived the day he brought dozens of balloons and kazoos to the orphanage. He had handed a kazoo to each child and motioned for them to watch him as he hummed into his. They all followed suit, spraying spit and slobber without song.

Laughing, he showed them again and again until the room vibrated with the sounds of joyful children blasting their tunes. Mai rolled over on her mattress and sighed, wondering why he hadn't come back for her as he promised. *Where was he now? Who would take care of her? Where was she going?*

Over and over again Mai asked that question. The answer, "America," was meaningless to her.

The next day she and the three hundred children were loaded onto a mammoth plane with dozens of volunteers. Again she asked the question. Again they answered, "America."

After several more plane flights and bus rides, the answer was, "Denver." Mai stepped off the bus with the other children and ascended a flight of stairs to yet another gathering place for the war orphans. She sulked into the room and heard a man call out breathlessly, "MaiLy!"

And there he was.

The American GI she had chosen in Vietnam ran to her, swooping her into his arms. He twirled her as she pressed her cheek to his in their familiar hug. He took her home that same evening, where she was welcomed by his wife, his two little girls, sugared Cheerios and Mickey Mouse sheets.

As she cuddled with her daddy on an overstuffed sofa, multicolored snowflakes glistened in the moonlight on the window pane. Sister Katrine was right: There are rainbows at the end of the storms.

LeAnn Thieman

The Girl with the Golden Hair

If you have anything against anyone, forgive him.

MARK 11:25

As twilight painted the room lavender, Sandy Moreno whisked a dust rag across knick-knacks. Reaching an angel figurine with a flaxen halo, she paused—and a train whistled in the distance.

You're still here, Tina, aren't you? Sandy thought as goosebumps danced across her skin. *Still working your miracle. . . .*

Three years previous, the forty-nine-year-old insurance agent was sitting beside her husband's bed in the ICU of Baylor Medical Center in Dallas. Mike had built their Honolulu cottage with his own hands, and even after he contracted hepatitis, you could find him surfing. But five years after Mike's diagnosis, he had deteriorated into complete liver failure.

"He needs a transplant," the doctors explained.

He will make it! Sandy felt in her heart. And Mike was in disbelief as he was placed on an organ waiting list.

"For me to get a new liver," he said, "someone must die." So they made a vow that after waiting the year required by the donor organization, they'd write and thank the donor family.

Finally, one stormy night five months later, doctors said: "We have an organ!"

Here's my chance, Mike thought as Sandy raced alongside his gurney.

For the next six hours, Sandy paced the waiting room. As morning broke, she bought a newspaper. *I'm too nervous to read,* she decided. *But I'll save it for Mike as a souvenir marking his re-birthday!*

Finally, the surgeon emerged. "That was the healthiest organ I've ever seen," he smiled.

Sandy felt excited, but at the same time sad: Someone had died for Mike to live. Yet that evening, Mike still lay in a coma.

"Why won't he wake up?" Sandy demanded.

"We don't know," doctors confessed.

Unable to sleep, sitting in a chair beside Mike's bed, Sandy picked up the *Dallas Morning News.* Her hands trembled as she flipped to an article about an eighteen-year-old girl who'd died when a train crashed into her car. There was a picture of Tina, her golden hair cascading over her shoulders.

Sandy bolted upright. She'd seen Mike's chart: His donor was a young woman. *This must be her,* Sandy thought. She glanced at the girl's youthful smile. Then she took her husband's hand. "You'll pull through!" she said.

After ten days and nights, Mike awoke—but he was babbling incoherently. Soon, an MRI revealed that Mike had central pontine mylenisis, a rare brain disorder.

"Maybe, with rehabilitation, he can have a normal life," the doctors said. "But there's only a 2 percent chance. . . ."

For the next two weeks, Mike struggled.

His right side was paralyzed. "You can do this!" Sandy urged him.

But after a month, Mike was still in pain. "I can't ... take ... any more!" he blurted. He looked at his wife. I've put her through enough suffering, he despaired. Maybe I should give up. Then he fell into a deep sleep.

Everything turned murky. *This is the end,* Mike realized. But then he felt a breeze—and saw a pinpoint of brightness. The light grew and grew. And from the illumination appeared ... a girl.

"Come on, Mike," she encouraged. "God wants you to live!"

Stunned, Mike peered into her face, at her twinkling eyes framed by short hair the color of honey.

"Who are you?" he stammered.

But the girl was already disappearing. "You can do it!" she sang.

She sounds like a cheerleader! Mike almost laughed, and he felt encompassed by a radiant warmth. Suddenly, he realized: *I can do it!*

The next morning, Mike said to Sandy, "I had a vision!" His eyes blazed as he continued.

"I saw a light, and this blond girl. . . ."

Sandy instantly recalled the photo in the newspaper, and she swallowed hard. *Could it be the same girl?* she thought.

"I want to get better," Mike stated with determination. Smiling, Sandy kissed his forehead. *Let him believe whatever gives him hope,* she decided. But she also resolved not to say anything about the girl in the train accident. *It may upset him,* she thought.

That day, Mike got into his wheelchair. Soon he was storming down hallways. The doctors were amazed. "There's no explanation for why Mike recovered," they marveled.

Sure there is, Mike thought. *I met an angel.*

Only a month and a half later, Mike went home 70 percent recovered, his new liver working well. A year later, he felt strong enough to surf again. Sandy told Mike, "It's time to write the letter."

You gave me a second chance, Mike penned. *Thank you.* Then he sent the letter to a national transplant organization, which sent it to his donor's family.

One month later, Mike received a letter postmarked Argyle, Texas. *We're the parents of your donor,* it read. *And we'd love to meet you. Signed Donna and Terry Minke.*

So Sandy and Mike flew to Texas. There, Donna presented Mike with a picture of long-haired Tina—and Mike gasped. It was the girl in his vision!

"I've already met your daughter," he began, trembling as he told them about his vision. "But she had shorter hair."

Donna's hand flew to her mouth. "Tina cut her hair after that picture was taken," she choked. "Before she . . . died in a train accident."

Sandy and Mike exchanged glances. The girl in the newspaper was Mike's donor!

"She was the youngest registered nurse's aide in Texas," Donna began. "And the day she got her driver's license, she said she'd checked off the boxes to be an organ donor."

"Tina was one heck of a third baseman, too," her dad chimed. "She even lobbied to get a softball diamond built. Her nickname was 'the cheerleader.'"

She was my cheerleader too, Mike realized. Then, placing his hands on his body, he said, "She's still doing wonderful things." Tina's parents fell into Sandy and Mike's arms.

Today, Mike is back to his old self, and the Minkes plan to visit him in Hawaii. In the meantime, they keep in touch. *How're ya feeling?* Terry writes.

Your little girl lives on, Mike writes back. And Sandy agrees. *Thank you, Tina, for your wonderful final gift,* she thinks. *You truly earned your wings.*

Eva Unga
Excerpted from *Woman's World* magazine

Waiting for the Bus

A man of many companions may come to ruin, but there is a friend who sticks closer than a brother.

To understand how I became acquainted with Minnie, you need to know about The Bus.

The Bus, as they call it, is the main source of public transportation around Oahu, the island on which Honolulu is located.

There are two kinds of buses on the line. The first is the early bus. It usually arrives a minute or two ahead of schedule, and no matter how fast you run, you can never catch up with it. The second kind is the late bus. It's a good idea to bring a book so you can read while you wait.

The ten-thirty bus that travels through Hawaii Kai, where I once lived, is a late bus. Fortunately, a stone bench provides a place to rest and relax while you wait. That's where I met Minnie. Twice each week I rode The Bus into downtown Honolulu. Minnie was a tiny, wrinkled Oriental woman in her late sixties or early seventies. Her hair was knotted at the back, and she always wore a muumuu, usually a dark color faded from years of wear. She carried an umbrella, not to protect her from rain, but to keep the sun away. Most days her umbrella was open when I arrived at the bench.

Minnie stored her valuables in one of those plastic bags you get at the supermarket. She must have done a lot of shopping because she had a different bag every day, or so it seemed. What she stored in those bags was a mystery, but the contents seemed important because she hugged the plastic bags close to her as we waited for The Bus.

The first day I encountered Minnie, she pretended I did not exist. It wasn't until the third or fourth time we shared a bench that she nodded when I arrived. By the seventh or eighth day, we had reached the "hello" stage. Once the ice was broken, small talk took over.

Minnie's conversational style was definitely local in flavor, a combination of the various types of pidgin English spoken in Hawaii. At first, it was difficult to follow. But once I became accustomed to the rhythm of her words, I could understand what she was saying.

Once we boarded The Bus, Minnie and I went our separate ways. It was as though we didn't know each other. She got off in the Kaimuki section, and I continued my trip downtown.

While waiting for The Bus, Minnie and I learned a lot about each other. She cleaned several condos in a nearby high-rise, which explained her presence in Hawaii Kai on a regular basis. I also discovered that she was a widow who lived alone in a small flat in Kaimuki.

"You're a Christian," she said one morning. "I saw you outside Holy Trinity Church when I went by the other day."

I nodded.

Her next words took me by surprise. "I used to be a Christian," Minnie said matter-of-factly. "I was baptized. Wish I still was, but I lost track of being one."

Much to my regret, The Bus showed up just then.

A couple of days later while we again waited on the stone bench, I asked her, "How come you quit going to church?"

"I didn't really quit," Minnie disclosed. "Things went against me, and I lost track of what it meant. My oldest sister lives over on the Big Island, and she says I should return to church. She gives me a lot of trouble every time I visit her."

Bit by bit and piece by piece, Minnie told me her story. Occasionally we discussed the weather, sports, politics and a variety of other subjects, but the conversation always came back to Minnie and the church. I will relate as best I can what she told me.

I had assumed that Minnie was Chinese. She was not. She was born in a small town somewhere near Seoul, Korea.

"My family," she said proudly, "was a good Christian family. All my sisters and brothers were raised in the faith. They grew up and married in the faith. I was the youngest, and I was preparing for my confirmation when the Japanese came. They took over my country. Most Americans do not remember that.

"There were soldiers in our town, and we lived in fear. We dared not go out at night, and when we did, we had to sneak down side streets and keep clear of the lights. Everything was locked up at night. You could not get into the church. The priest lived in fear of his life. The Japanese were watching him, and he had to hold his services in secret.

"I hated the Japanese. The soldiers were cruel and made life difficult for all of us. They didn't beat us, but they filled us with fear and ordered us around, shoving us if we did not hurry. I still shiver when I think of those soldiers.

"One night I went to the church and asked the priest about my confirmation. He warned me to be careful and said that he would let me know when confirmation would be held for the children in our town. That was the last time I saw him. Some said that he had fled to the hills when the Japanese came to arrest him one night. Others said that he was dragged away to a prison camp. Our priest never came back. The years went by, and the war ended. The Japanese went away, but I was never confirmed.

"By then I wasn't young anymore. I had grown up. I married a man who didn't share my faith. I lost track of my religion.

"My first husband died, and I came here to Hawaii. I married again, but we lost our only child in a fire. Later, my second husband died. I have been alone for several years.

"I hate the Japanese," Minnie concluded. "If they had not been so cruel, I might have grown up in the religion of my family. I'm an old woman now. I'm too old to go back."

I explained to Minnie that age had nothing to do with it. I think I was beginning to get the message across to her that day when The Bus came along.

On another day I arrived at the stone bench to find Minnie hugging two plastic bags. "Things I use for cleaning," she explained. "I won't be coming back to the condos anymore."

"Did you lose your job?" I asked.

"Not me," said Minnie with pride. "I quit.

I'm moving to the Big Island. My older sister's husband has died, and I'm moving there to be with her. My sister's a Big Boss. She'll make me jump. Goes to church every day. Wait and see, she'll make me do the same thing."

A warm glow filled Minnie's eyes, and a look of contentment settled on her face. For the first time since I had met her, Minnie looked beautiful.

The Bus came then, and we climbed aboard. I never expected to see her again.

Several months later I spotted a sweet little lady, all spruced up, sitting on the stone bench waiting for The Bus. It was Minnie—without her plastic bags.

"I figured you'd be along," she greeted me. "It's Tuesday. You always take The Bus on Tuesday."

Minnie had been visiting one of her former employees in the high-rise. "I came to Honolulu to see my eye doctor," she informed me. "Need new glasses. Came to see old friends, too. You're one of them."

I was pleased. For the first time since we'd met, Minnie and I let The Bus go by that morning.

"I got big news," she said. "Big, big news!"

"What is it?" I asked quickly, figuring she had remarried.

"I'm a Christian now," she said. "God has welcomed me home again."

"That's wonderful, Minnie!" I exclaimed.

"There's something else," she said.

"What?" I wanted to know.

"To join our church," she said, "I had to go to classes. I don't read or write well. A little woman about my age helped me."

"Yes?" I said, a bit puzzled.

"She was a little Japanese woman who came to Hawaii about the same time I did," Minnie went on. "She was so kind, so good. I don't believe I would have made it if she had not been my friend."

Minnie paused to let what she had said sink in, and then she asked, "Know what?"

"What, Minnie?"

My friend did not hesitate. "Maybe I don't hate the Japanese anymore," she said, and she was smiling. "Maybe I'm beginning to like them. Maybe that was why God made me wait so long before he welcomed me home again."

Minnie and I took The Bus downtown

together that day. Letting go of her hatred had transformed her.

Richard W. O'Donnell

Who Is Jack Canfield?

Jack Canfield is one of America's leading experts in the development of human potential and personal effectiveness. He is both a dynamic, entertaining speaker and a highly sought-after trainer. Jack has a wonderful ability to inform and inspire audiences toward increased levels of self-esteem and peak performance.

In addition to the *Chicken Soup for the Soul* series, Jack has coauthored numerous books, including his most recent release, *The Success Principles, How to Get From Where You Are to Where You Want to Be* with Janet Switzer, *The Aladdin Factor* with Mark Victor Hansen, *100 Ways to Build Self-Concept in the Classroom* with Harold C. Wells, *Heart at Work* with Jacqueline Miller and *The Power of Focus* with Les Hewitt and Mark Victor Hansen.

Jack is regularly seen on television shows such as Good Morning America, 20/20 and NBC Nightly News.

For further information about Jack's books, tapes and training programs, or to schedule him for a presentation, please contact:

Self-Esteem Seminars
P.O. Box 30880
Santa Barbara, CA 93130
Phone: 805-563-2935
Fax: 805-563-2945
www.chickensoup.com

Who Is Mark Victor Hansen?

In the area of human potential, no one is better known and more respected than Mark Victor Hansen. For more than thirty years, Mark has focused solely on helping people from all walks of life reshape their personal vision of what's possible. .

He is a sought-after keynote speaker, bestselling author and marketing maven. Mark is a prolific writer with many bestselling books such as *The One Minute Millionaire*, *The Power of Focus*, *The Aladdin Factor* and *Dare to Win*, in addition to the *Chicken Soup for the Soul* series.

Mark has appeared on Oprah, CNN and The Today Show, and has been featured in *Time*, *U.S. News & World Report*, *USA Today*, *New York Times* and *Entrepreneur* and countless radio and newspaper interviews.

As a passionate philanthropist and humanitarian, he has been the recipient of numerous awards that honor his entrepreneurial spirit, philanthropic heart and business acumen.

For further information on Mark's products and services, please contact:

Mark Victor Hansen & Associates, Inc.
P.O. Box 7665
Newport Beach, CA 92658
Phone: 949-764-2640
Fax: 949-722-6912
FREE resources online at:
www.markvictorhansen.com

Who Is Patty Aubery?

Patty Aubery is the vice president of The Canfield Training Group and Self-Esteem Seminars, Inc. and president of Chicken Soup for the Soul Enterprises, Inc. Patty has been working with Jack and Mark since the birth of *Chicken Soup for the Soul*.

Patty is the coauthor of *Chicken Soup for the Surviving Soul: 101 Stories of Courage and Inspiration from Those Who Have Survived Cancer, Chicken Soup for the Christian Soul and Chicken Soup for the Expectant Mother's Soul*. She has been a guest on over 150 local and nationally syndicated radio shows.

Patty is married to Jeff Aubery, and together they have two wonderful children, J.T. and Chandler. Patty and her family reside in Santa Barbara, California. Contact:

Patty Aubery
The Canfield Training Group
P. O. Box 30880
Santa Barbara, CA 93130
Phone: 1-800-237-8336
Fax: 805-563-2945

Who Is Nancy Mitchell Autio?

Nancy Mitchell is the director of all copyrights and permissions for the *Chicken Soup for the Soul* series. She works closely with Jack and Mark on all of the *Chicken Soup for the Soul* projects.

Nancy coauthored *Chicken Soup for the Surviving Soul: 101 Stories of Courage and Inspiration from Those Who Have Survived Cancer, Chicken Soup for the Christian Soul* and *Chicken Soup for the Expectant Mother's Soul.*

Nancy resides in Santa Barbara with her husband Kirk. Contact:

Nancy Mitchell Autior
P. O. Box 30880
Santa Barbara, CA 93130
Phone: 800-237-8336
Fax: 805-563-2945

Contributors

If you would like to contact any of the contributors for information about their writing or would like to invite them to speak in your community, look for their contact information included in their biography.

Richard Bauman has been a freelance writer for over twenty-five years. His articles about spirituality, history, travel and self-help have appeared in numerous national publications. Richard and Donna, his wife of thirty-eight years, reside in West Covina, California. They have two adult children and three grandsons.

Lini R. Grol is a Canadian citizen from the Netherlands, who has published poetry, stories, plays and illustrations in books and periodicals in the Netherlands, the United Kingdom, Belgium, South Africa, the United States and Canada. She received the Canadian Authors Award from the Canadian Club of Hamilton Ontario.

Tim Madigan is a senior feature writer for the *Fort Worth Star-Telegram* newspaper in Fort Worth, Texas. He lives with his wife,

Catherine and children Patrick and Melanie in Arlington, Texas. His email address is *tmadigan@star-telegram.com*.

Mayo Mathers is a columnist for *Virtue* magazine, contributing editor for *Today's Christian Women*, and a freelance writer who has contributed to nine books and coauthored *Like a Pebble Tossed* and the *Legacy of a Prayer*.

Roberta L. Messner is a quality-management specialist, author and inspirational speaker. She has written over 100 articles, which have appeared in over 100 different publications, as well as two books. Her work has appeared in other *Chicken Soup* books and she is a regular contributor to *Guideposts* and *Daily Guideposts*. She is also a field editor and photo stylist for a number of home-decorating publications.

Richard O'Donnell has had articles appear in a number of anthologies, most notably those published by Yankee, Inc. and Smithsonian. He currently is working as a freelance writer and enjoys collecting old-time radio shows. Richard considers himself a short story and movie buff.

Sean Patrick has published his family-oriented series in *Catholic Digest* since 1987. His stories about his Irish-American family have been published in a book, *Patrick's Corner.* A former deputy sheriff, he now lives in rural retirement in the heavily Amish area of northeast Ohio.

LeAnn Thieman is a nationally acclaimed speaker and author and a member of the National Speakers Association. LeAnn inspires audiences to truly live their priorities and balance their lives physically, mentally, and spiritually while making a difference in the world. She coauthored *This Must Be My Brother.* You can contact her at *LeAnnThieman.com.*

Eva Unga writes for the *Woman's World* magazine.

More Chicken Soup?

We enjoy hearing your reactions to the stories in *Chicken Soup for the Soul* books. Please let us know what your favorite stories were and how they affected you.

Many of the stories and poems you enjoy in *Chicken Soup for the Soul* books are submitted by readers like you who had read earlier *Chicken Soup for the Soul* selections.

We invite you to contribute a story to one of these future volumes.

Stories may be up to 1,200 words and must uplift or inspire. To obtain a copy of our submission guidelines and a listing of upcoming *Chicken Soup* books, please write, fax or check our Web sites.

Chicken Soup for the Soul
P.O. Box 30880
Santa Barbara, CA 93130
fax: 805-563-2945
Web site: *www.chickensoup.com*

Also Available

Chicken Soup African American Soul
Chicken Soup Body and Soul
Chicken Soup Bride's Soul
Chicken Soup Caregiver's Soul
Chicken Soup Cat and Dog Lover's Soul
Chicken Soup Christian Family Soul
Chicken Soup Christian Soul
Chicken Soup College Soul
Chicken Soup Country Soul
Chicken Soup Couple's Soul
Chicken Soup Expectant Mother's Soul
Chicken Soup Father's Soul
Chicken Soup Fisherman's Soul
Chicken Soup Girlfriend's Soul
Chicken Soup Golden Soul
Chicken Soup Golfer's Soul, Vol. I, II
Chicken Soup Horse Lover's Soul
Chicken Soup Inspire a Woman's Soul
Chicken Soup Kid's Soul
Chicken Soup Mother's Soul, Vol. I, II
Chicken Soup Nature Lover's Soul
Chicken Soup Parent's Soul
Chicken Soup Pet Lover's Soul
Chicken Soup Preteen Soul, Vol. I, II
Chicken Soup Single's Soul
Chicken Soup Soul, Vol. I-VI
Chicken Soup at Work
Chicken Soup Sports Fan's Soul
Chicken Soup Teenage Soul, Vol. I-IV
Chicken Soup Woman's Soul, Vol. I, II